UKULELE MANUSCRIPT BOOK

I0810180

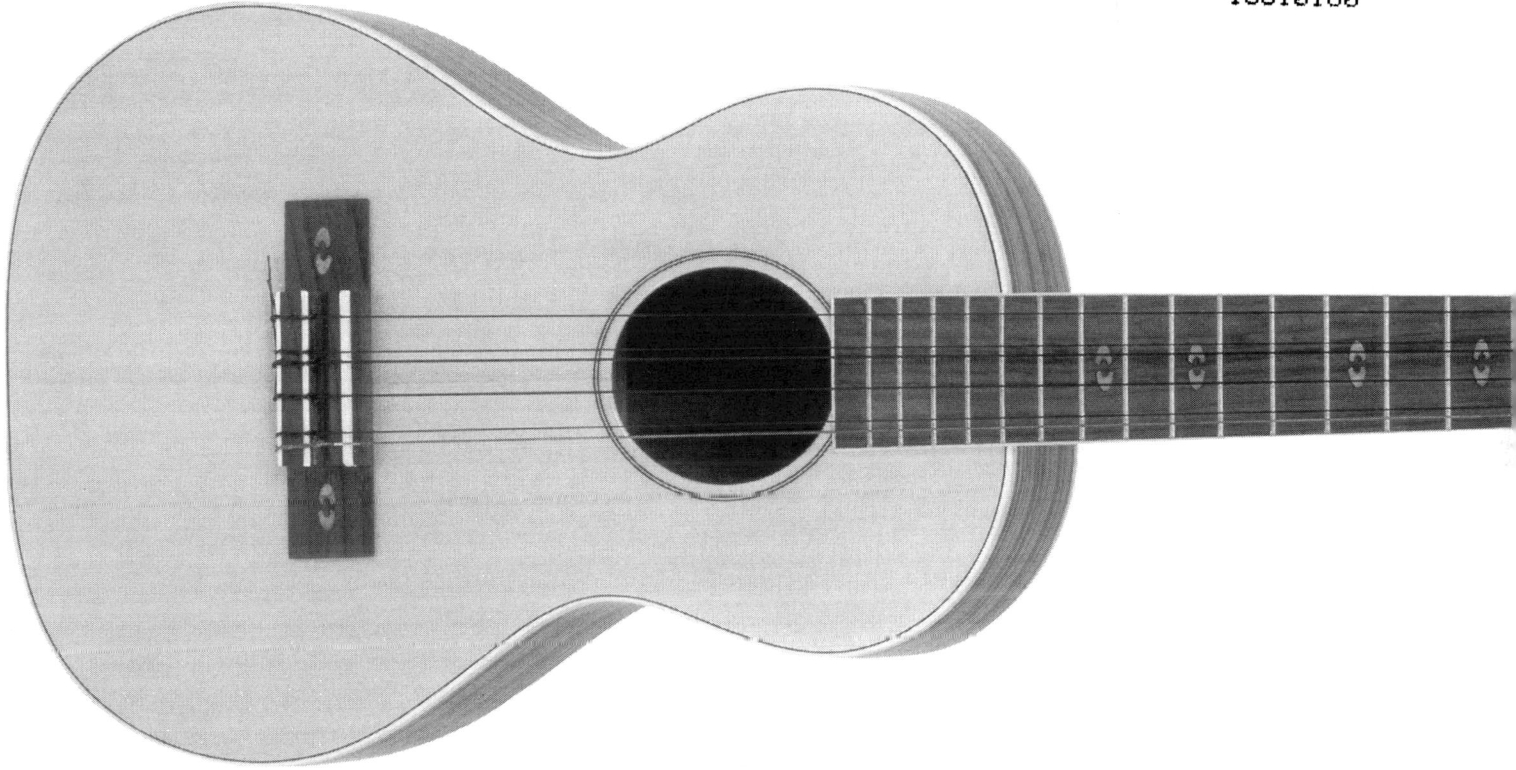

Cover & title page photo by George Moore, courtesy of Hohner, Inc.

MEL BAY

© 2011 BY MEL BAY PUBLICATIONS, INC. ALL RIGHTS RESERVED.

WWW.MELBAY.COM

MEL BAY PUBLICATIONS, INC.

MEL BAY PUBLICATIONS, INC.

MEL BAY PUBLICATIONS, INC.

MEL BAY PUBLICATIONS, INC.

MEL BAY PUBLICATIONS, INC.

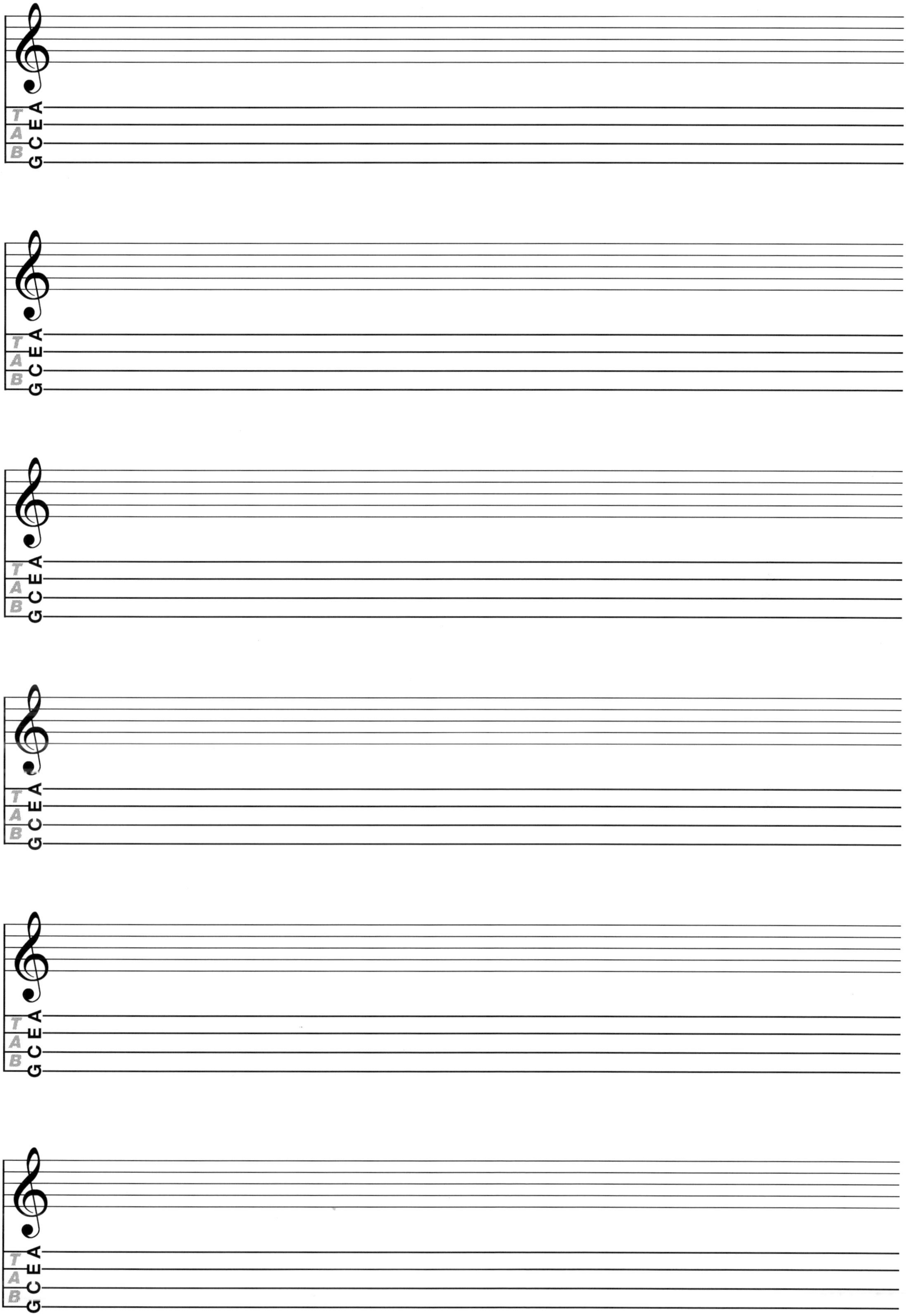

MEL BAY PUBLICATIONS, INC.

MEL BAY PUBLICATIONS, INC.

MEL BAY PUBLICATIONS, INC.

MEL BAY PUBLICATIONS, INC.